Be the Master of your life

Think For Yourself
By

Victoria Elias

This document must first have permission from the publisher before being copied or otherwise reproduced.

Introduction

Introduction

Your intellect is your biggest asset.

Your life will be defined by the way you think. The power of our imagination is limitless. For instance, Einstein only utilized around 1% of his mental capacity, yet look at what he was able to accomplish.

This book will teach you how to think for yourself and free yourself from the influence of other people's ideas and opinions. It will show you how ideas form, develop, and ultimately lead to decisions about what to do.

You can and will be liberated from other people's attempts to sway your opinions.

You will develop the ability to think independently, benefiting only yourself.

Rich and powerful individuals who have a vested interest in how and what you think run the world. They employ mass media, influential leaders, and advertising as their tactics.

Independent thinkers won't be sufficiently impacted by anything mentioned above. They will use their reasoning skills to act in their own best interests.

You are being taught how to think in this book.

We will make fewer mistakes and lead easier lives if we learn to think. This is because you can remove the majority, if not all, of the emotions from a situation by thinking things through before acting. You'll have more self-control and serenity. You put your mind and cognitive process on hold when you respond and only act on your emotions. The same is true for decisions; on average, a decision based on emotion will be 99% incorrect.

Many issues in your life can be resolved by learning how to think before you act or make a decision. When you went to school in the past, you were taught how to think critically and to consider all options. The best debater could construct a convincing case for both his own position and the opposing one. In my opinion, students are being taught what to think rather than how to think. Radical thought and behavior are the results of seeing only one side. Their mind is no longer free; instead, it is being held captive by a single or a group of concepts. Their thoughts are confined.

They can never get anything from this.

We hope that after reading this book, you would reconsider how you think. This book's goal is to accomplish that.

Also keep in mind that you can adopt either a culture that operates above the neck or below the waist. Your decision.

Chapter 1

The Benefits of Thinking for Yourself

There are three sorts of minds, the open mind, the accepting mind, and the closed mind. Any concept or opinion will be taken into account by the open mind, but only after being thoroughly examined. A constrained variety of thoughts and concepts are also acceptable to the accepting mind, which will accept them wholeheartedly and without hesitation. What concepts and ideas are genuine and true has already been decided by the closed mind.

Any concept or notion that is in opposition to these predefined thoughts and ideas will be rejected by the closed mind.

People who choose to think independently—and this is a decision—will be open-minded. They will give their imaginations total freedom to explore each and every idea through to its logical conclusion, both positively and negatively.

They'll let their brains go wherever they like.

No self-restraint, bigotry, or prejudice will be tolerated. Any emotional concern, whether favorable or bad, won't sway it. Emotion, bigotry, and prejudice will be defeated by logic and reason.

By allowing your mind to think in this manner, you will give yourself the best opportunity to choose the course of action that will serve your interests.

You will be liberated from notions and thoughts that others will try to force on you in order to further their own interests if you think for yourself.

You won't be forced to follow any philosophy or belief.

Your mind will be free to adapt to any changing conditions that may exist at any given time.

Nobody will ever be able to call you a closed-minded person.

You'll have the freedom to think for yourself, which will enable you to live a free life devoid of illogical worries.

Because you will be able to accept things as they are and be able to see yourself and others for who they truly are, you will have the highest opportunity of experiencing true peace of mind.

Instead of being limited to the hypothetical realm of would, could, and should, you will be able to live in the actual world of is.

Those who uncritically adopt the beliefs, ideologies, and concepts of others will suffer as a result. They have no thoughts of their own, thus their lives are empty.

These are the advantages of using your own judgment.

You can decide how to think for yourself or how to think for other people.

Chapter 2

Where Thought Starts

You must be aware of what is in your subconscious mind since that is where thinking starts and where it begins to develop. One of the finest ways to achieve this is to reflect on your actions after you have done them and ask yourself, "Why did I do this?" You'll ask yourself a question, but you'll immediately realize the answer isn't the underlying cause. It's possible that you'll keep asking yourself "Why did I do this?" until you discover the true explanation for your actions.

Your subconscious mind has informed you that this is the genuine cause, and although it may not be appealing or pleasant, it is the one that has been occupying your subconscious as well. You'll eventually learn what is in your subconscious mind if you keep doing this process with every action you take. Your subconscious mind is the origin of your impulses. You'll start to understand who you are and what caused the thought or thoughts to enter your head.

The conscious and subconscious halves of our thoughts are separate.

In essence, they are viewed as two halves of a single consciousness.

It's possible to compare the mind to an iceberg. The subconscious, or the other 90% of the mind, is below the water and invisible, while the conscious mind, which makes up roughly 10%, is above it.

Our conscious mind, which primarily consists of choice, volition, awareness, learning, suggestion, and logic, is what we are aware of.

We become what we imagine and tell ourselves to be.

The suggestions are made by the conscious mind, and the thoughts are carried out by the subconscious mind.

Every action has a tendency toward self-preservation, and the subconscious mind controls this mechanism.

The life within our bodies is under the control of our subconscious.

It unconsciously causes the heart to beat, our lungs to breathe in and out, our digestion system to take the food we eat and turn it into energy and eliminate it, and for the heart to pump oxygen, energy, and nutrition to every atom, molecule, cell, and tissue every few seconds for the entire 24 hours of the day.

The instinct, ethic, conscious, or sensory component of the conscious mind is where the suggestion of the conscious mind starts.

The recommendations are either accepted or rejected by the subconscious mind.

Once the inhibitions against it have been overcome, the subconscious will implant it if it is accepted. It will first be ingrained, after which it will be impressed in the subconscious and transmitted to a nerve center. The suggestion develops into an impulse once it reaches the nervous system. It results in action, a reaction, and finally, reality after becoming an impulse or a series of impulses.

As a result, what exists in your subconscious mind impacts what happens in the outside world. What then exists in our subconscious mind becomes the question. First of all, our subconscious stores every experience we have had—what we have seen, heard, felt, and done.

The subconscious acts as a self-preservation mechanism and might shield us from remembering certain memories. In essence, our subconscious functions as a computer that stores, classifies, organizes, and retrieves data in order to solve problems. The unlimited life energy is connected into this subconscious mind computer. This might explain why we only employ 1% of our mind. The subconscious has essentially infinite power. Only those with special vision can do the unthinkable. All of the information we have seen, heard, read, or felt is stored in our subconscious, which has the capacity to instantly transform any or all of the aforementioned into an idea.

We do have the ability to use our brains freely and explore somewhere that nobody else has gone before.

Last but not least, we are protected by our subconscious mind, which operates in self-preservation mode. Any influence or impression—positive or negative—that has been made on us results in a conditioned reaction. A collection of conditioned reactions make up our personality and who we are. This combination of conditioned reflexes and our subconscious mind will dictate what and how we think.

Instinct

What happened in the past and the effects it had on you are the sources of instinct. Everything you do or feel is stored in your subconscious mind. It serves as a repository for your emotions and the effects they have had on you. You probably aren't aware of the effects of what has happened because your conscious mind is not able to remember everything that has happened to you. Deep inside of you, instinct alerts you to danger or a positive sensation about something. Because instinct has a fundamental influence on what you have seen, heard, tasted, odored, and touched, as well as how your views have been shaped by all of the above, instinct should not be disregarded.

Your instincts can alert you to danger or point you in the direction of something that will be helpful to you. These instincts are set up by your mind for your benefit, and part of how you think is to pay attention to them.

Impulse

The three sources of impulses are nerves, instinct, and ethics. Additionally, they come from your conscious and sensory regions of the mind; after they have made an impression on your subconscious and nerves, they will develop into impulses. Accepting an urge or impulses causes action, reaction, and ultimately reality.

Impulses are the beginning of the actions you will take and should not be disregarded. They will serve as the foundation for your varied emotions. You'll finally act on your impulses.

Your nerve system and mind handle all of this. Impulses have a big role in your thought process. In other words, your thoughts will shape your reality, for better or worse. The first step in thinking is accepting and comprehending your instincts and inclinations. What you believe and how you think will shape your life.

Asking why we think the way we do is the first step in learning how to think. Everything starts with an instinct. We first experience a thought, then an impulse. "Now where did the impulse come from?" is the query.

Was it something we saw, felt, heard, or experienced? Or was it something we read, heard, or experienced? Was the impulse a good or bad one? Impulses are crucial because they frequently lead to action. When it all comes down to it, thinking is essentially just asking questions. Knowing how and where an activity began becomes crucial because the results of our activities will determine how our lives turn out.

It all began with an urge. Asking yourself "where did this impulse come from" over and over again will help you maintain control over your thoughts, your behavior, and ultimately your life. You must continuously asking so that you can recognize the right response when it comes to you.

Response and Action

Keep in mind that impulse leads to action. The nerves that are driving this movement frequently press an emotional button; these feelings include anger, sadness, joy, and a wide range of others.

An emotional response is brought on when this occurs.

Because of the lack of thought involved, reactions can be poor.

The decision-making, learning, and reasoning processes have been disregarded, and the action is solely emotional. Fortunately, if we want to employ it, the mind does contain an inhibitory factor. Our inhibition mind, which will tell us to pause and consider, can be activated by our instinct and choice minds. Our rational mind begins to function when we start to pause and ponder, asking questions like, "What would happen if I do this?

What would happen if I make this emotional choice in the end?"

The rational mind is also aware that decisions made only on the basis of feelings are typically poor choices with disastrous results. The key is to stop and consider before acting when you are about to do something because of an emotional response.

One of the steps in developing autonomous thought is doing this. There will be less issues and a higher quality of life if you develop the habit of utilizing your head rather than acting on your emotions and thinking rather than reacting.

Chapter 3

Confront Yourself

The courtroom is where disputes are settled. Both the for and against arguments will be presented by each side. Anyone who wants to think independently and independently must be able to develop a strong case for their position in any debate or clash of ideas. The independent thinker must then be able to create a counterargument that is just as compelling.

A debate team needs to be able to make a case for something they were previously opposed to. You must be completely open-minded and willing to let go of some long-held beliefs in order to do this. In other words, you need to be able to consider opposing viewpoints. If you cling to concepts or beliefs that have taken control of your mind and imprisoned it, this is not feasible. You'll have locked up a portion of your mind in a cell and lost the key. The mind of an independent thinker must be unrestricted in order to consider all notions and ideas.

If your thinking is influenced by your emotions, this is difficult. Your mind will no longer be free and your thinking will be anything but independent if you allow yourself to become a prisoner of your emotions.

You must be able to allow both perspectives to enter into any thought or concept. Although it is difficult, doing this is vital if you want to use your intellect to its best potential. All of this is a component of independent thought.

Chapter 4

Robotic Mind

You have turned into a robot if your thought process can be summed up in a two-word phrase like the Vietnam War's "Hell no, we won't go," which we witnessed people screaming in unison on the streets. The person or group that implanted this two-line motto in your head is in control of you. They now own your mind.

Your mind will soak up what they say and believe like a sponge. You have a sincere faith.

You'll probably die with the person's or group's opinions, ideas, and beliefs still fresh in your mind. Except for their ideals, you will have had a closed mind your entire life. Your time is being completely wasted on this. Perhaps if you had used your brains to the fullest extent, you could have accomplished amazing things.

Your mind is like an advertisement that is played repeatedly in a store to sell goods, so you will never know. The sponge of your mind is just as brief as these adverts.

You are being utilized without even being aware of it; you have transformed into someone or some organization's robot.

If you lose out on experiences that only your mind could enjoy, you'll probably live a life that is wasted. If someone or something controls your thoughts, you won't have contributed anything to anyone else.

Welcome to robot country.

Chapter 5

Four Pieces to a Puzzle

When you purchase a puzzle, you receive a box of pieces that you must assemble to reveal the entire image. You cannot finish the puzzle if any component does not fit in the designated spot. You'll have four corners after you're done. Usually, you'll try to start at the corners and move inward. Now let's propose that the puzzle is a problem, a difficulty of

any kind, rather than a puzzle. Whatever the case, this issue has the same four corners, which are:
What are you aware of?
2. What do you not understand?
3. What you must understand
4. What do you hope to learn and accomplish?
To finish your solution, you must first begin moving into the center of your problem. Each of the four questions must have an answer. The puzzle-like nature of the problem means that it cannot be solved if any piece is left missing.
Let's start by asking you when the issue first started, given what you know about it.

What kind of issue is it exactly? Do you possess the ability to resolve it? Do you genuinely want to fix it? What additional individuals or inanimate objects, such as metals, liquids, and other similar objects, are involved? What unites the animate and inanimate worlds, what is the common concern? What do you not understand?

Exist any occurrences that you are unaware of? If there is a problem with the persons involved, do you know who they really are? What element would be required, if it's a thing problem, that may or may not be present?

What information is required? If it is a people issue, you need to be aware of what each person stands to gain or lose, as well as their history and way of thinking. You must be aware of their history, state, and aspirations for the future. If there is a problem with a thing, you need to know its tolerance, for instance, the composition of metals, and which inanimate object gets along with which other one. You still need to know more than what is presented here.What do you want to know, why do you want to know it, what will you learn or accomplish, how will the problem be solved help you, and whose problem is it?

When dealing with others, especially, you could discover solutions to the problem that you didn't know about and don't necessarily like but that are necessary. If certain things are involved, you can discover that you either overestimated or underestimated their strength or tolerance, and that you were unaware of their genuine characteristics. You might have to accept your own shortcomings. To solve the issue and discover the truth, you might need to view things from a different perspective.

There is no such thing as a straightforward issue.

An illustration of the puzzle's four corners

You can think of every difficulty as a puzzle. Like a jigsaw, problems are made up of numerous pieces, and if any one of them is missing, the problem cannot be fully solved. If one of the pieces of the puzzle is missing, the picture will never be complete. The same holds true if a puzzle piece is placed incorrectly. Placing the four corners in place and starting to work inward is how we solve problems. It does call for careful thought, close scrutiny of each component, and a complete lack of presumption.

We'll take beginning a new business as an example of the issue.

We start by responding to the question, "What do you know?"

Part 1: What do you know

You are aware of the type of business you want to launch. You are aware that money must be spent. You are aware that you need to be knowledgeable. You are aware that there is a possibility for the company to collapse.

You are aware that you will require assistance in some way, whether it be financial or from knowledgeable individuals. You are aware that it will take some time for this firm to get off the ground. You are aware that until the business becomes self-sufficient, you will require a source of revenue.

You are aware that in order to launch your firm, you will need the help of your family and friends. You are aware that the likelihood of failure rises in the absence of such assistance. You are aware that this will be a teaching moment. You are aware that mistakes will be made. You are aware that some of these errors will cost you money. You are conscious of your limited resources. You are aware that the success or failure of this company primarily rests with you.

Part2: What You Don't Know

The initial expense of doing this is unknown to you.

You are unsure about the company's precise location. The amount of your rent is unknown.

You have no idea how many workers you might require. You are unsure of the amount you will give them. You have no idea who or how many providers there are. You have no idea how much business you will generate. The amount of money you will make or lose during the initial phase is unknown.

You never know what kinds of personnel issues you might encounter. You have no idea where or how to seek the assistance you require.

You have no idea how many expenses will arise that you had not budgeted for.

You don't know where to promote or how much money to spend on advertising. You are unsure of the price tag on your advertisement. What effects your advertisement will have is unknown. You are unaware of the identity or location of your rivals. What your staff will do is unknown to you. You don't know how much it will cost to finance your company or who will provide that financing. You have no idea how many rules and regulations the government may issue, let alone what you will need to do to comply.

You are unsure of what you will ultimately sell—your goods or services. After deducting all of your costs, you are unsure of how much to charge for your good or service. You are uncertain about your personality or managerial skills.

Part 3: What Information Is Required?

You need to be aware of the location of your company. You must be aware of your rent obligation. You must be aware of the startup costs for your firm as well as the costs for the first year.

There is a proverb that reads something like this:

Determine how much it will cost to operate your company for a full year. Determine your projected revenue for the first year of operation, and then multiply that number by two to get your projected operating costs. If you divide the anticipated revenue you would have in the first year in half, you will probably be quite close to the actual amount.

You must understand how to interact with employees. You must be aware of the payment amount. You must be clear about the type of employees you require. You must understand how to pay them.

You must be aware of a reputable CPA's name. For your business, you must be aware of all governmental rules. You must be familiar with legal requirements for employees. Knowing when to pay your employees is important.

If you require finance, you need to know which bank to use and how much assistance they will provide. You need to be aware of what your partner or pals think of your endeavors. You must be aware of the extent of your family's or friends' support. You must determine the price that you will charge for your goods or services.

You must determine who will provide you with the products you need to operate your firm. You must be aware of those vendors' prices.

To guarantee your success, you must be aware of how much of each good you will require. You must be aware of a reliable attorney's name in case you ever need one. You must have a plan in place in case you fail.

Part: 4. The Information You Want

You're interested in finding out the answers to every query in #3 and more. To accomplish all of your goals, you must first understand what they are, how you plan to accomplish them, and when you believe you can complete them.

Will you be satisfied if you accomplish these goals?is something you should be aware of.

Conclusion

As you can see, problems are made up of a variety of components and elements that you must be aware of, consider, and keep piecing together until you find a solution. If you ever hope to find a solution to an issue, you must think creatively. You must make no assumptions and weigh every possibility.

Chapter 6

How and Why

Two reasons exist. While the other cannot be replied, the first can. The why that can be answered will be easier to respond to if you know how to reason.

When a person inquires, "Why do good people suffer bad things?" or "Why did they leave us while they were so young?" These why questions are of a spirits character and are beyond our intellect or understanding, hence there is no clear solution to them.

A young woman in her fifties was in the final stages of stage 4 breast cancer. Every week, a large family gathering would take place at the residence. They would question her why this is happening to her or why she is leaving us at such a young age as they sat around the table. It was an ongoing procedure.

When someone finally spoke up, they stated, "We are not meant to understand, therefore even if God were to come down right now, sit at this table, and explain in minute detail why this happened, you would still not understand. It is of a spiritual character, which is forever outside of our control.

If we spend any time trying to understand the why behind a spiritual topic, we will just waste our time and energy while becoming upset. The physical reality in which we live is a factor in the why question that can be answered and typically does require an answer. Whether organic or inorganic, animate or inanimate, questions like why a building's side suddenly caved in or why one chemical won't mix with another are common.

Due to their inherent curiosity, young kids will occasionally inquire as to why something occurred. When someone responds with an explanation, the youngster will ask "why did that happen?" and when someone responds with a different explanation, the child will ask "why did that happen again?" This continues indefinitely until the adult gives up or provides the solution. A child who asks "why" repeatedly is thinking for himself and not just accepting whatever response is provided to him. When we inquire why, we're trying to figure out the answer or the real story. You must evaluate each response and discard any that don't make sense or fully address the question if you want to think for yourself.

If we want to be able to think independently, a lot of questions must be addressed and thoroughly analyzed.

Finding the truth or the bottom line is not simple. People who want to think for us generally avoid asking "why" inquiries.

Keep in mind that your mind is your own and that only you have the authority to decide what to think.Once more, there are some problems that cannot be addressed since the solution is beyond the scope of our intelligence. There are certain "why?" inquiries that have an answer and can be answered. Someone might say, for instance, "This problem cannot be solved." "Why not?" is the response that someone with independent thought will provide.

Until the truth is discovered, the why not question will be posed. Someone with independent thought will not accept false explanations. Our minds should be utilized, not misused.

Chapter 7

The Purpose of Life Is Gain

One big game is called life. Everyone wants something for themselves, and everyone else wants something from you. Everyday people play this game, and those who can't think for themselves will lose. People will remark that he is quite wealthy. Unless the person is a counterfeiter, this is not true. In actuality, we take money rather than making it. The people who take the most money and use it to seize the most power are the true victors in the world we live in. When someone or any group gives you an idea, a philosophy, or something they claim to be true, the only reasonable thing to do is to ask yourself, "what do they expect to gain from what they are saying"?

Do they want you to "buy" what they are saying in order for you to accept it and support their cause, or do they want you to provide money in order for them to support their cause and increase their power and wealth? If there is a fair trade, taking money from other people is generally not a bad idea. Quick for Quick. Contrarily, conmen take from you and give little to nothing in return, whether it is with regard to your cash, your body, or your intellect.

The issue appears when someone speaks or behaves in a way that serves their own self-interest. You stop thinking and accept what they say without considering or asking what they stand to gain. These requests for favors are frequently made from an emotional place. Your emotions override reason, causing you to believe what they are "selling." You are being manipulated without even being aware of it.

They have something they want, and you don't even know what it is since you haven't used your mind's power to question and consider what they would stand to gain by using logic.

There are people in this world who want to take over your thoughts so that you would accept their worldview. Once more, you are a tool. Thus, the question is: How can a person guard against having their thoughts taken over by someone else or some other entity? To believe nothing and to doubt everything is the first rule. What some people claim to be facts may only be speculation. It does not become true just because someone says it is true.

They could need you to believe the "fact" in order to advance their goals. Anything that is presented as fact should always be questioned, and you should think about what and how they stand to gain if you accept it as true. Accepting these "facts" if you accept their premise is almost too convenient. Your worst adversaries are now your own thoughts and the conventional wisdom. It might be too difficult or uncomfortable to raise a doubt or adopt a different viewpoint. You can choose to use or lose your mind.

Perception

We tend to believe what we see. For a significant portion of the population, perception has become reality. Perception is simple. It doesn't require any planning or work. When we see something that resonates with our values and feelings, we accept it exactly as it is. A man could come out as sincere, courteous, and honest. This shapes the way we see the man. We take as truth what we have seen. This is our opinion, which we own.

If we spend enough time with this man, his true self might emerge. It constantly does. Once we are able to perceive him for who he truly is, our perspective shifts and we are exposed to reality.

Does this imply that we will start to look at and take into account what is actual rather than what we believe to be real? Most likely not. When we can adjust our views and personalities to how we see the world, it appears much better. Sometimes it's hard to find the truth. We now have to accept what is actual rather than what we would prefer to perceive as real, which requires mental effort.

Even though reality occasionally tastes really bad and is unpleasant, it is nonetheless true. Although the truth will set you free, not everyone aspires to be liberated. There is too much accountability. We favor making up our own worlds.

A more pleasant, trouble-free, and satisfying world. Then, if you want to use it, the mind enters the picture and modifies our perception. If we decide to use it, our mind has the capacity to provide us with a choice. We have the ability to make decisions.

Chapter 8

The Would, Could, and Should World

This is a unique planet. Whatever you desire it to be is possible. It is a world devoid of difficulties and issues. It is a universe in which everything is just as it should be. Everyone should act justly, honestly, and peacefully in this world. Your kids should be respectful, considerate, loving, and academically successful.

Your husband needs to be reliable, dependable, and let's not forget, hardworking. Friends should stand by our sides and support us in good times and bad. Our parents should support us in everything we do and treat our partner with the same affection as their own child. No one should go without, and things ought to be better. Drugs should not be condoned, and criminals should be punished for their wrongdoing. These are only a few examples of what ought to be.

The realm of possibility also includes statements like, "I could acquire a better job if I had more schooling, patronized the boss, or wasn't placed in a dead-end employment.

My kids could do better in school; if the teachers were fair and impartial, they would take more time to support them or be more accepting of their personality.

If my spouse knew the proper people and didn't speak out for himself, he may earn a promotion. If my spouse made more money, if I had fewer issues with the kids, and if my in-laws weren't so critical and intrusive, I may be happier. My husband and I would be more affectionate and considerate if I had more free time to myself. If I had a finer house, a better area, and some new furniture, I could be happier.

If I could just get out of this rut I'm in, everything would be perfect.

If it weren't for all the corrupt politicians and avaricious businesses, things would be better. If there was less materialism and people cared more about one another than they did stuff, the world would be a better place. Without all the drugs, the world would be a better place. If we all just attempted to get along with each other, things would be better. If things weren't so intricate and confusing, we may be happier.

There is no such thing as the realm of would, could, and should. It is an invention of your imagination and only exists in your head. It is a vivid dream that we can see whenever we want to. Although it is our wish, it rarely becomes a reality.

All of us exist in two universes. The universe of would, could, and should exists alongside the world of is. It is and remains what it is. It is reality's world. This reality is unchangeable by us. We may change the world, but first we must accept it for what it is—not for what we wish it were, could be, or ought to be. The fundamental truth is known to our consciousness. We either chase after it or reject it. Although we have the ability to alter what we can and accept what we can't, we also have the ability to accept things as they are.

We have that option when we think for ourselves. Let reality take over from delusions.

Chapter 9

Our Changing Mental State

Everyone is experiencing some kind of mental condition. Either we are all hypnotized or not, depending on the situation. Most people are unaware of the fact that we occasionally experience high suggestibility. When we are in this state, verbal or nonverbal recommendations can readily penetrate our minds and ideas, influencing or controlling us without our knowledge.

We will heed advice from others and, to some measure, submit to their authority. There are people with specific objectives in some professions, such as advertising, self-help seminars, public speaking, politicians, or TV product salespeople. Be aware that their intention is to use the fact that people are frequently in a hypnotic state to persuade them to "buy" whatever it is they are "selling" -- whether it be a service, an idea, a philosophy, or a perspective on the world. Control of the mind.

So how do we know that this is happening and that we are being influenced even though we aren't aware of it? One method is to become aware of the automatic behaviors we engage in without even realizing it. Examples include tapping your fingers, crossing your legs while moving your foot back and forth, vacant staring, rubbing your hand over your face, etc. The list goes on, but the main idea is that you are engaging in behaviors that you are not consciously aware of. We refer to this as hypnosis.

Realize and acknowledge that you are prone to having your mind influenced and that you are being used or are about to be exploited when you find yourself doing without thinking.

What are they "selling" and why, you might wonder.

You can think independently rather than being influenced by others by having just one simple notion.

Because your mind is yours and not someone else's, you will be aware, and you must be attentive.

Even when you sleep, the process of entering and exiting hypnosis continues. R.E.M. refers to the state of heightened suggestibility that you enter when you lose control. This means that whenever you move your eyes, your eyelids will flutter. You enter a dream state when your eyelids start to flutter. At this time, dreams occur.

Every night you dream, but most of the time you don't remember them.

You will have a fair probability of remembering your dreams if you tell yourself each night just before you go to sleep, "I will remember my dreams." A dream is a reflection of your subconscious, and it can provide you insight into what is happening there.

Chapter 10

The State of Mind

If you have a positive perspective, one of your mind's most potent tools is your mindset. A mindset might be neutral, good, negative, or any combination of the three. A mindset is a collection of self-suggestions paired with unwavering conviction that dispels any skepticism. Consistent success builds the mindset until it becomes an unstoppable and unstoppable force.

A person has the ability to overcome an immovable force when they are truly motivated to succeed.

People having the mindset of trying to manipulate others for their own personal gain and benefit do so. Leave no room for ambiguity. Ever since the dawn of civilisation and even before, there has been a battle. This conflict is one of the mind.

We will suffer if we don't think with the power of our minds. You can have the freedom to be your own person if you have a positive outlook and refuse to let anyone or any organization dominate your mind in any way.

On the other side, a pessimistic outlook will make your life a nightmare of failures and unhappiness. Positive or negative options are yours. Another option is to choose to be indifferent. This mentality makes the decision to not think at all. Your thoughts will be muddled up like a leaf in dirt. Your thoughts won't be focused or directed in any way. One of the strongest strengths of the mind is the power of believing, which the optimistic attitude possesses.

You can do things you never imagined imaginable if you can sincerely believe without any doubt whatsoever. It is entirely up to you to decide.

A Stare

People with the intent to dominate, intimidate, or control us have the mentality necessary to achieve just that. They employ a variety of strategies, but they always work toward the same end—intimidate, dominate, then control. One technique they use for this is the stare, which involves staring somebody in the eye. It is known as gaze control.

You can make someone or a group feel less, weak, and inferior when you can look them in the eye. They are in a position to influence people's thoughts and convince them to accept their ideas, philosophy, and beliefs if they are able to accomplish this. It is possible to shield yourself from this spell.

You must first develop the mindset that you will not allow anyone to dominate or control you. When someone is trying to dominate by staring, their eyes will flicker from one to the other. Focus your attention directly between their eyes whenever you are in their company. Avoid seeing them in the eyes.

With the idea that you are in charge, fix your gaze on a location directly between their eyes. Their eyes are darting back and forth; they will never be able to stare you down. They'll start to blink.

They will also sense the strength of your thoughts and gaze. You will be astounded by the outcomes of this one straightforward procedure. You may use it with the strength of your mind.

Chapter 11

The well-organized mind

The organized mind is based on two main tenets.

The first rule is to create compartments inside the topic or issue. Sort everything out. The second rule is to set up the compartments in ascending priority. An illustration would be moving into a vacant home that requires repairs and is overflowing with clutter that was left by the previous owners. You start by organizing the debris into containers.

Let's take as examples the clutter on the outside, in the kitchen, the bathrooms, the bedrooms, and the attic. After categorizing the clutter, you must pick which items are most crucial to get rid of and which are secondary, then you must start the clutter removal process.

Repairs are the next thing to think about and compartmentalize, after which you should separate what has to be done, such as replacing or repairing the roof, the floor, the stairs, the basement, the plumbing, etc. It is necessary to determine the priority of the tasks at hand.

The third area to think about is the furniture you will need for your home, including items for the kitchen, living room, bathroom, and bedroom as well as other items for decoration.

Establishing the hierarchy of priority is necessary. So, let's break down how to set yourself up for success in this circumstance.

1. Since you cannot start making repairs until the clutter is cleared away, you have determined the sequence in which it should be eliminated.

2. Start making the necessary repairs in the order of importance.

3. Once all repairs have been made, arrange the furniture according to importance after choosing it.

Your life must be well-organized or it will be in complete disarray. You are asked to deliver a speech,

for instance. Your prepared remarks must first be organized. Give a ranking of priority to each area or topic that needs to be covered.

Following completion of this, each area or subject should be documented. The three elements that must be included are the introduction, the conclusion, and the comedy, in that order of significance. You must use humor, otherwise your speech would be flat. If you can add humor to each category, your speech will be successful if you have correctly categorized each subject.

In order to build an order of priority, your mind must first categorize the information.

When your mind is structured, it will perform better in every single aspect.

Chapter 12

Making Decisions

When you make a decision the first question you have to ask yourself is, "Was this decision based on emotion or a logical premise?" If the decision was made only out of emotion, it was probably a mistake that was afterwards regretted. How long did it take me to get to this decision? is the other crucial question to ask.

Did you thoroughly consider all of the alternatives? In each of the possibilities, both pro and con, did you ask yourself, "What will happen if I'm wrong and what is the best I can expect to achieve?"

Did you ask yourself, "what will happen if I'm wrong" with your final decision? Did you make a hurried decision or did you take the time to evaluate all of the ramifications and consequences be they pro and con?

If you stop to think about it, practically every minute we are awake, we are making decisions like, "Should I get up now?" and "After I get up, what is the first thing I need to do?" along with "What am I going to eat for breakfast, and what will I do first after I eat?" What attire do I intend to don today?

Despite how insignificant they may seem, every choice has an impact, such as when you choose to wear inappropriate attire or eat something at breakfast that causes indigestion. The questions keep coming, such as "What school should I go to, should I get a divorce, should I buy something I can't afford," in addition to the decisions you make every minute. Every choice, no matter how big or small, should be carefully considered. This is one of the main causes of your mind's need to consider all possible outcomes before making a choice.

The key question is: "Am I going to use my mind to the fullest extent, or am I going to live my life just making decisions at random?" Or, even worse, allow someone else to direct your thoughts or make decisions for you. It's in your head. It is not anyone else's.

Chapter 13

Imagination

The entertainment hub of your mind is your imagination.

When you read a book, especially one that is fiction, your imagination takes over and you see things in your head like bustling streets, lovely cottages in the woods, an elderly woman with a cane, etc. This helps you relax and puts you in a good mood. In a nonfiction book, particularly one about a biography or even a book on mechanical or chemical processes, your imagination may even start to operate.

Chemical processes or how pieces fit together can be observed. It's dreadful to let your imagination go to waste.

You can picture a dismal future, war, going hungry, falling prey to a ruthless gang, or any of the above. These imaginative journeys can make you feel scared and anxious. Being anxious is like being enveloped in an ominous fog; all you know is that it is unpleasant. A person who is experiencing fear or anxiety is simple to manipulate or influence. To manipulate or control us, someone must first instill dread or anxiety in us.To do this, mind control is employed.They want to have power over us so they can have control over where we live.

They provide us assurance with a grin and let us know what they will do or accomplish for us. Then they start forcing us to act in automatic ways, such as raising a clenched fist or repeatedly saying a word. They then start limiting our options by telling us what we can and cannot do.

People will become separated because those who disagree with them will be painted as villains. Divided we fall; united we stand. Last but not least, they remove the restraint they had placed us under, causing those who had been restrained to lose control and anarchy to break out. Then they have a justification to seize all power in an effort to put an end to the chaos and regain order. Such a system of law is complete control. Only those who are incapable of thinking or who do not utilize their minds to think can experience this. When a person thinks independently, they are better able to discern people who would like to have influence over their thoughts.

They can visualize this outcome using their imaginations. It's not difficult to imagine what life was like in Nazi Germany. This has been carried out in the past. Mind control's guiding concepts are not new. Their will has been put to the test throughout time. Your creativity holds the key. You have the capacity to look past the here and now and envision what lies ahead.

Your imagination and mind are both yours. Be wary of anyone who wants to dominate your thoughts and imagination for any purpose.

.

Chapter 14

Free Your Mind

I don't even want to think about it, how often have you heard that? You have restrained your thoughts and put them away when you say this. Putting your head in the sand is the topic here. You block out the fact that something horrible is about to happen, nearly ensuring that you will end up a victim.

You decide to become a victim and let things happen. Clearly, this is a mistake. The greatest thing to do in a circumstance is to think about the worst case scenario and start preparing for it. You must accept what will happen if there is nothing you can do to prevent it. Either act or accept. All of this occurs in your head. In any circumstance, we have the option of being positive or negative. We must open our minds, not close them or put them in a state of restraint.

A person who has a closed mind has not only restrained but also caged their mind. We will have more control over our life when we liberate our minds since we will be able to think of all possible scenarios. Even in the worst situations, we can choose to be optimistic. When we let our minds go wild, we are free to recommend only positive things about people or circumstances and to refrain from suggesting anything bad. Beyond your wildest dreams, your mind is powerful.

Because we are in charge of our thoughts rather than suppressing them and limiting their scope, our lives will be better. Instead of having someone put a leash on your mind, lead you around to their way of thinking, accept their ideas, act on their behalf, and close our mind to anything else, you will start to be free and think for yourself. Political correctness could be used to describe this. When you unleash the power of your mind, you can do and achieve things that you could never have even dreamed about.

You and who you are are in your mind. Release the strongest force you possess. You are always free to choose. Utilize it or lose it.

Chapter 15

Having the upper hand

We all interact with people and events in one of two ways throughout our lives. We will either negotiate from a position of strength or weakness. When we deal from a position of strength to a position of strength, whether actual or imagined, we can employ our brains. The imagined component was created by the power of your mind. Dealing from a position of strength will offer you the ability to influence the majority of circumstances and have control over your life, whether that strength is genuine or imagined.

You'll be able to alter your environment. The imagined can come to life in your thoughts. It won't be obvious if you truly believe this and possess the authority of a mindset that puts you in charge. Your projected strength will be taken as genuine. Your adversaries will make the erroneous assumption that it is real. As a result, the game is now in your favor. It is unknown if the strength you portray is genuine.

You can use this position of strength in any aspect of your life, whether it is actual or imagined.

It will make a difference in how you deal with people, groups, and the regular everyday situations that come up in everyone's lives. By using the power of our minds to think whatever we choose to, we have the strength to do this.

You won't be able to take genuine control of your life if you don't use the power of your mind and decide not to think. Your mind will naturally choose the route that presents the least amount of difficulty. Your mind will have a propensity to take in other people's concepts and thoughts. The term "weak-minded" has a specific meaning.

No matter who or what you are, your mind has the power to decide to behave from a position of strength. There's always going to be a choice.

Jumping Off a Cliff's Edge

A buddy of mine recently shared with me the beginning of his wholly altruistic organization for cancer patients. There were many donors who were eager to see the group get off the ground. To raise a significant sum of money to launch it, they began a fundraising effort. They only succeeded in generating less than $5,000 after a month of intensive fundraising.

The donors became quite agitated and worried. They were giving up and declaring it a lost cause.

Since it was a subject that was dear to their hearts, they were upset and were quite emotional. They let their feelings dictate their actions, and as my friend put it, "they were all jumping off the end of a cliff." When your mind becomes closed up and you are unable to reason or comprehend the prospect of a positive outcome, this is what happens. They would have spared themselves and everyone associated with the project a great deal of emotional distress if they had used their minds to consider that there might still be a beneficial conclusion.

In the end, the charity received almost $170,000 after donations started to come in. That's more than they required.

Negative thoughts make it difficult to control our feelings.

We are unable to think clearly when our emotions are in charge.

The difficulty arises at that point because we have lost the ability to come up with a solution because all solutions are the result of thought. A issue justifies looking for a fix.

Chapter 16

Your Children Should Learn to Think

One of the most priceless things you can give your kids is the ability to think for themselves. Their life will be altered, as well as the course of it. It could mean the difference between them succeeding in what they do and failing to know what to do. The ability to think independently can also influence one's mental outlook and interpersonal interactions.

You can't rely on the classroom to instill critical thinking in kids. Depending on the political climate of the school district, it is more probable that the school will instruct students on how to think.

Biased political ideologies, philosophies, and views shouldn't be taught in schools, but they are in some of them. This is why a child or adult should use their own judgment rather than letting prejudiced notions and beliefs soak into their minds, which only serves to benefit those who stand to gain from individuals who accept these ideas and views.

Giving a youngster examples that they can relate to and understand is one of the finest ways to teach them.

A person with two boys could serve as an illustration.

They are warned to arrive home at a specific time or face dire repercussions. I don't know what the serious repercussions would be, but I don't want to find out, one boy reflects. The other boy acted in accordance with his desires and stayed out later than was appropriate without considering the repercussions. Due to his maturity and careful consideration, the youngster who returned in time was awarded. The other boy simply acted and did what he felt like doing; he didn't stop to ponder. For a month, he was also "grounded".

The cost of being unthinking.

Consequences must be taught to children.

That is because there will be repercussions for everything you do. They must be educated to consider the repercussions of their actions before acting. Will there be positive or negative effects? A youngster can learn the fundamentals of thinking for himself once you can educate him what repercussions are and how to consider before you act in order to avoid negative outcomes.

The same applies to acting and responding. A child is using his thoughts when he is taught to consider his actions before taking them. When the child is educated that negative outcomes will occur if he behaves without thinking and simply reacts emotionally.

This child needs to be educated that everything has two sides and that he must consider all the information available—both positive and negative—on each side. You will have given your child a solid foundation for independent thought if you can teach them these three fundamental ideas and help them realize that everything has consequences, that there is a difference between acting and reacting, and that there are usually two or more sides to every story. Additionally, it needs to be emphasized to them that while they will always be free to make decisions, they will also have to live with those decisions.

Chapter 17

Our ideas shape how we perceive the world.

A concept is a broad idea or comprehension that is developed from particular instances or happenings. a concept or idea.

Our fundamental conceptions serve as the foundation for our senses and general way of thinking. For example, if we receive a ticket for exceeding the speed limit while maintaining the speed limit, this incident will cause us to have a poor opinion of law enforcement in general.

This has an impact on our impression since we now see police as being unfair and have a bad opinion of them. Most of our ideas are derived from our experiences. Any encounter we have will leave us with a concept, either a favorable one or a negative one. When we reflect, we realize that having negative beliefs and views is not in our best interests. They will have an impact on our mental health, but first we must be aware of them.

To do this, we must think, or else we risk becoming paralyzed by unfavorable ideas and thoughts.

Other ideas emerge as a result of our acceptance of the thoughts, values, and philosophies of other individuals, groups, or organizations.

We are "sold" these ideas. There are ideas for practically anything. You must critically evaluate each idea you have and be honest with yourself about how you came to that idea if you want to think for yourself. Have you "sold" it, or have you acquired it naturally? Is the idea constructive or destructive?

Do you feel good about having it or bad about having it?

And do you just socialize with others who have the same ideas, or are you willing to examine ideas that are in opposition to your own?

In our imaginations, we reside. Concepts determine whether you'll have a joyful or miserable mental state of affairs.

Make a decision after giving it some thought, as only you have that authority.

Chapter 18

Understanding and Knowledge is Power

What is learning?

What you are aware of and have in your head is knowledge. Do you base your understanding on actual events or what someone has told you? How did you learn this information—from a book, a lecture, a friend, or from personal experience?

The response will aid in determining how reliable the knowledge is. The source of the knowledge in a book depends on who wrote it and how they learned the material.

How biased a lecture is and what they stand to gain if you choose to believe what they are saying will determine how much you learn from it. Knowing anything from a buddy might be highly shaky because it might be hearsay or rumor. It might even be true.

Experience is another source of knowledge, and since it is direct, it is perhaps the most trustworthy. You need to consider what knowledge you want to store in the vault of your mind. You are what you believe you are. What are you going to do with all of this knowledge now that you have it? Are you going to share it with someone or keep it to yourself? Do you want to learn things for your own benefit and to obtain power, or do you want to learn things to serve others? a generous act?

The more experience you have, the more information you get.

Your perspective on the world, other people, and yourself changes as your knowledge grows. When you make independent decisions, you must be conscious of the changes in your life and the knowledge that is behind them. You can choose how you want to use all of the knowledge you have by opening the knowledge vault in your mind and taking a look inside.

Chapter 19

For The First Time

There is a proverb that states, "You will mess up anything you do the first time." Most of the time, this is accurate, but not always. Before doing something for the first time, we should consider the best strategy to make it successful. What am I going to need to make it successful? What do I need to understand to succeed at it?

What if I don't succeed?

Why is it necessary to understand everything mentioned above? Because we will always be doing things for the first time, from childhood until old age, we should always consider things through, especially while doing them for the first time. Our entire lives will be spent trying things out for the first time. Our earliest actions and perspectives determine whether we succeed or fail in life. We have an option if we fall short. This failure might be seen either positively or negatively.

We can choose to see this as a benefit by using the power of our minds. You could say, "Hopefully, I gave it my best effort and picked up some new skills. I believe I know what I did incorrectly, therefore I will try again in the hopes that I will do it correctly the following time. So you continue to try.

You can also opt to view things negatively. "Nothing I do is right. I'm terrible at anything I try. Everything works against me. I have failed. When you start to believe this, your mind's strength will enable you to bring it about.

Life is filled with firsts. Usually, you can try to repeat what you did previously. Failure can be transformed into success if you have the appropriate mental attitude. Think independently and don't be swayed by people who want you to fail because they are also failures and are always yearning for company.

Chapter 20

Never blink

Every person on the planet will experience a crisis once in a while. Two different types of crises exist. The first crisis is a natural one, while the second crisis is artificial. You have to realize that there will be natural disasters, but you can "keep your head on" if you employ your mind's thinking capacity.

Consider: What is the first and most crucial action to do?

You must then ask yourself, "What else do I need to do?"

You can overcome this natural crisis if you think and don't blink. Do not let fear consume you. Nobody can think for you in a circumstance like this, so think for yourself.

A man-made crisis is the opposite type and can be either political or economic. Both of these were the result of human activity, and those responsible stoked the fires of disaster for their own political or financial advantage. They are not bothered by the problem, nor are those who knew about it and stood to gain from it bothered by it. The only people it affected were those who weren't expecting it and were caught off guard. The majority of them were paralyzed by fear and worry.

Their lives slipped out of their hands. Anxiety and fear seized control. They fell prey to them.

You need to use your own judgment in situations like this to avoid being a victim. It is most important for those who caused this situation to feel scared and afraid.

People who are scared or anxious are much simpler to manipulate. Make use of your intellect and consider the situation's reality. If I just keep my cool and don't blink, how will this affect me?

The first action you take is this. This provides you some time to consider what would be the best course of action given the current situation. Refuse to be duped by propaganda.

"What actions can I take which will benefit me the most?" Those who are knowledgeable have mastered this. People who are gripped with fear and worry should not be listened to. You have the option to avoid being a victim. You have the option to make your own decisions.

Chapter 21

Having an Open Mind

"Humanity longs to be big and acknowledges its smallness; it seeks happiness and acknowledges its misery; he would prefer to be perfect and realizes that he is full of flaws; he would prefer to be the object of men's love and regard and realizes that his flaws only justify their dislike and disdain. He develops the most unfair and criminal desires imaginable as a result of his embarrassment because he develops a fatal hatred for the truth that accuses him and exposes his flaws.

Everyone of us has a mind. Our attitude, who we are, what we believe, and how we live are all influenced by it. One who has an open mind is thought to be one who will pay attention to and weigh the truth of what they observe or hear. A person who is truly open-minded will weigh all of the arguments without bias. They will base their decision on validity and actuality. This is a mind that has independent thought. It is completely impartial and devoid of any bias. There is also the open mind, which accepts everything or most of what they see and hear without any reservations, especially if it has an emotional appeal.

Consequently, this becomes their "truth." Every other piece of information is untrue.All at once, they have entirely opened their mind and then completely closed it. They have encircled the mind in a circle that is impenetrable.

No matter what, everything in that circle is real. Outside of that circle, nothing is real. The circle will accept any concept, notion, or conviction that will strengthen what they already see as true. Nothing will even be somewhat considered that is outside of this circle.

In a short amount of time, they went from having an entirely open mind to having an entirely closed one.

Chapter 22

Original Thought

Who is the original thinker and where does he start thinking in an original way? Original thought has a start but no finish.

The unreal, or what is currently nonexistent, is where original thought originates. If the thinking is already in existence or has been expressed by others, it is not original.

When the mind imagines a universe that doesn't exist, original thinking begins. A world of unrestrained imagination.

No original thinking or ideas can exist if the imagination is restrained. When a concept, philosophy, or belief is rotated through 360 degrees, each angle is analyzed, processed, and subjected to the ultimate test of what would happen if utilizing the imagination to consider the outcomes of each situation. This is when original thought can start. You can start by being creative yourself.

To use an example, consider asking yourself, "In my wildest dreams, what would I think if I had the genius of Einstein? "You are capable of going inside yourself and opening your consciousness. Or possessed limitless strength or lacked any sort of emotion?

What if I had the capacity to observe everything occurring on Earth from above?

When you think independently, your mind is capable of original thought.

Chapter 23

Control Your Mind

Focus. Focus is the essential component of any discipline. Focus comes before goals in terms of value. Goal is followed by method, and mindset comes last but not least. We have to teach our minds to think first. Positive outcomes are the only options available.

If our way of thinking is negative, we won't be able to concentrate, and if we can't concentrate, discipline is difficult. We will be able to pinpoint our objective once we have a constructive focus. Instead of just having a disciplined mind, our objective is to have a strong mind that is resistant to accepting emotional and/or deceptive statements, no matter how illogical they may be. A feeble mind is also susceptible to ideas, beliefs, and ideologies that have no basis in reality and are propagated by a group in order to further their own objectives.

Our thoughts need a method to distinguish between the true and the false by carefully examining the facts and asking only the questions that are accurate and realistic. The attitude is the final component of mental discipline and is essential to the balance of all the other components. Everything is held together by the thinking, which acts like cement. The attitude is fixed in place and unaffected by any outside influences. You can only develop mental discipline if you have your own opinions. You alone are capable of developing and upholding mental discipline. We need to have complete faith in our ability to control our thoughts. If we decide to use it, we have the ability to make this happen. Your decision.

The majority of the propaganda that affects the public is driven by goals chosen by a small group of people whose identities we do not know and will never know. The group mind does not actually think in the way that we do. Rather, it is influenced and directed by impulse, feelings, and previous experiences, which are conditioned responses, also referred to as conditioned reflexes, or knee-jerk reactions. Any propaganda attempt will succeed or fail depending on what the public wants.

On the other hand, propaganda has the power to arouse desire.

The fundamental question now is: How do people who wish to think independently and take charge of their lives navigate this onslaught of information?A rundown of the positive, negative, and ugly. We can only choose what knowledge is necessary for us to know and evaluate its value.

The other option is to adopt the collective mindset and accept that we are part of the herd. Your decision still stands.

Conclusion

You have a clear choice now that you are aware of the options accessible to you for how your mind can function.

You have the option of choosing your own thinking or letting other individuals, groups, etc. decide for you.

If other people or groups dominate your thoughts, and you embrace their ideas, beliefs, or philosophies, you are no longer free. You will undoubtedly end up being a victim and are most likely being used. You may take charge of your life by thinking for yourself.

Let there be no doubt, we are attempting to sell you the idea of thinking for yourself, but you are being given a choice. You are left with no other option by the misinformation and other sales tactics. They must have their way or not at all. We would like to thank you for purchasing the book and for reading it.

We can only hope you found it enjoyable and maybe even picked up a few new things. This book has accomplished its goals if it has benefited even one person.